BIG Fun 3

WORKBOOK

Mario Herrera
Barbara Hojel

Big Fun
Workbook 3 with Audio CD

Pearson Education, 10 Bank Street, White Plains, NY 10606 USA

Staff credits: The people who made up the **Big Fun** team, representing editorial, production, design, manufacturing, and marketing, are Isabel Arnaud, Rhea Banker, Danielle Belfiore, Carol Brown, Kim Casey, Tracey Munz Cataldo, Dave Dickey, Gina DiLillo, Christine Edmonds, Erin Ferris, Nancy Flaggman, Yoko Mia Hirano, Penny Laporte, Christopher Leonowicz, Emily Lippincott, Maria Pia Marrella, Jennifer McAliney, Kate McLoughlin, Linda Moser, Kyoko Oinuma, Leslie Patterson, Sherri Pemberton, Salvador Pereira, Pamela Pia, Juan Carlos Portillo, Jennifer Raspiller, Aristeo Redondo, Nicole Santos, Susan Saslow, Kimberley Silver, Jane Townsend, Kenneth Volcjak, Lauren Weidenman, and Carmen Zavala.
Text composition: Isabel Arnaud
Illustration credits: A Corazón Abierto

Printed in USA
ISBN-10: 0-13-3445275
ISBN-13: 978-0-13-344527-5
11   17

PEARSON ELT ON THE WEB

PearsonELT.com offers a wide range of classroom resources and professional development materials. Access course-specific websites, product information, and Pearson offices around the world.

Visit us at **www.pearsonELT.com**.

CONTENTS

BIG FUN
Song

Chorus ➔

From the sky to the ground
And all the way around—
We can have big fun!
If there's rain, if there's sun,
Let's play with everyone.
We can have big, big fun!

Take a walk outside.
Our world is big and wide.
There are flowers and trees
And yellow bumblebees.
Buzz, buzz, buzz!

(Chorus)

Join your hands with me.
Let's see what we can see!
Then take a closer look.
We'll learn beyond our book.
Look, oh, look!

(Chorus)

1 AT SCHOOL

What is wrong? Find and circle.

Draw the English teacher and the principal.

cat

PRINCIPAL

SECRETARY

Vocabulary Practice: *English teacher, music teacher, principal, secretary*

Look and match.

Vocabulary Practice: *gym teacher, janitor, gatekeeper*

✂ Cut out and paste. Draw yourself and color.

Vocabulary Review: *bus driver, music teacher, bus, classroom*

Look and circle the correct letter. Trace and draw.

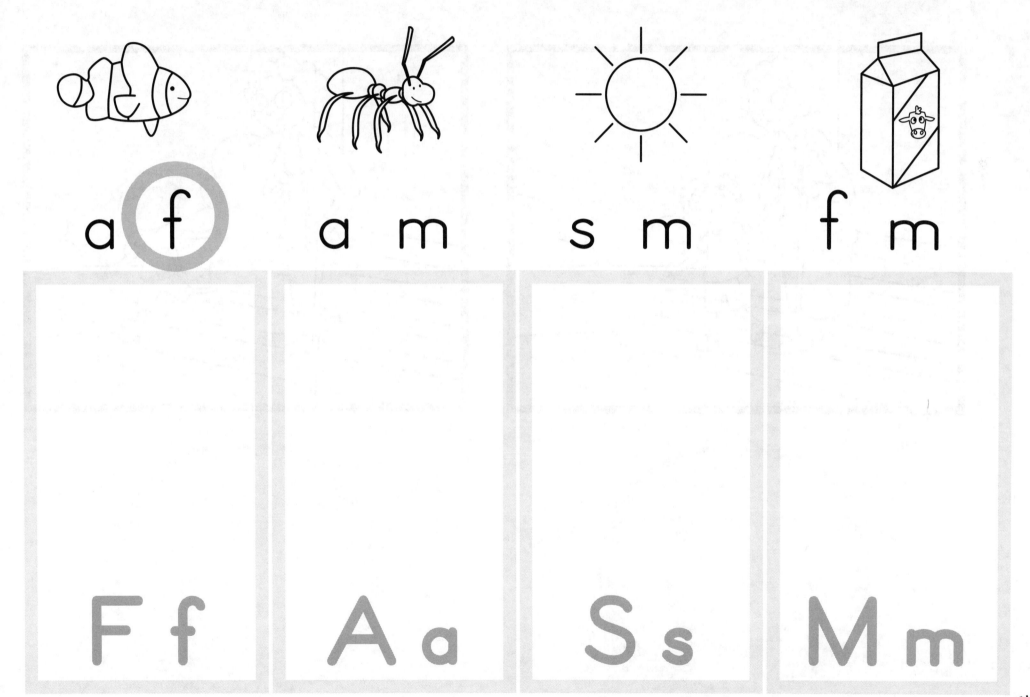

a (f)   a m   s m   f m

F f   A a   S s   M m

VALUES

Look, trace, and draw a happy face or a sad face.

Values: We respect others.

Listen and point. Listen again, match, and trace the numbers.

Who Is She?

1

2

3

4

Count, draw and trace. Color.

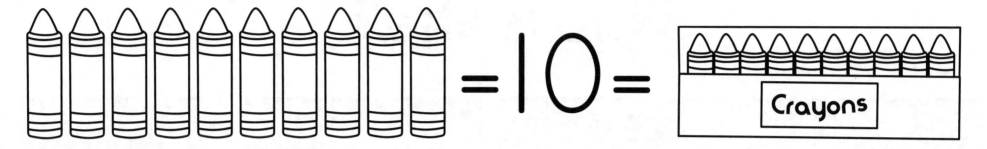

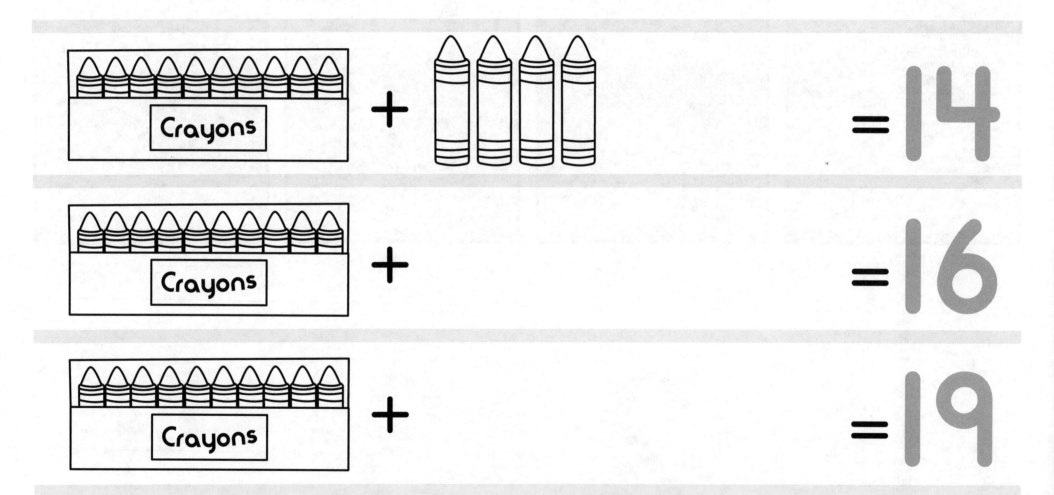

Math Practice: *Numbers 1–19*; sets of 10

What does each animal make? Look and match. Color.

Amazing: Science Connection: *cow, milk, bee, honey, chicken, eggs, sheep, wool*

UNIT 1
9

AT SCHOOL

Draw people at school.

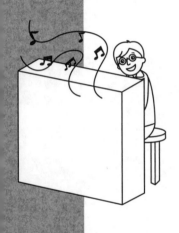

2 FEELINGS

What is wrong? Find and circle.

Look and color the matching face.

Vocabulary Practice: *sleepy, happy, sad, amazed*

Look and match.

Trace and draw actions that make Mom mad and happy.

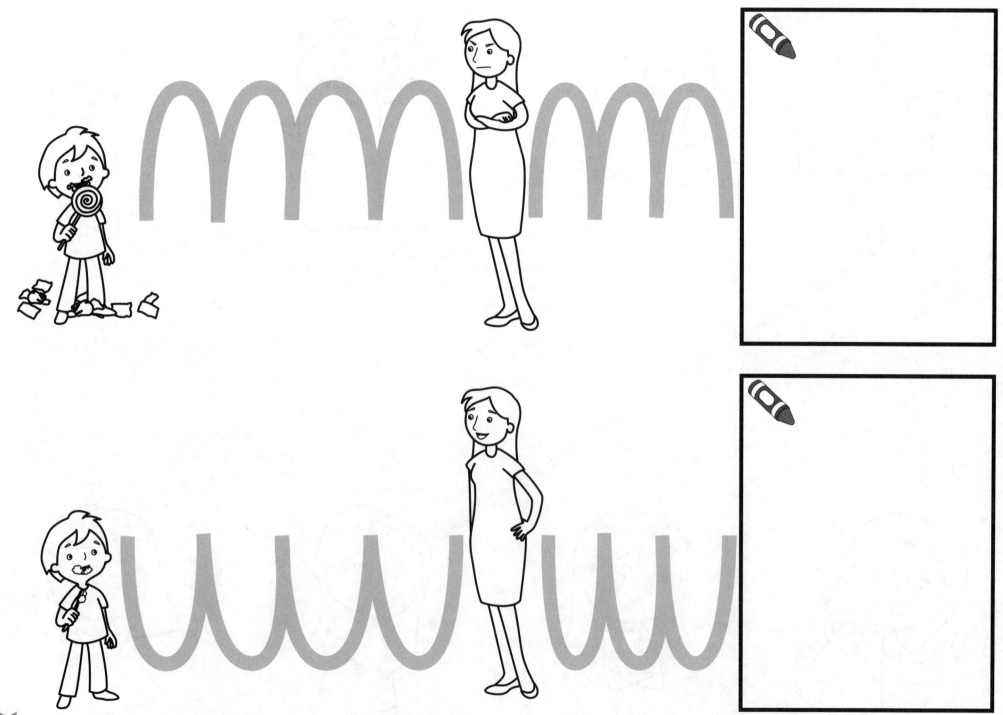

Vocabulary Practice: *eat unhealthy food, brush my teeth; mad, happy*

Look and circle the correct letter. Trace and draw.

l t

p l

e t

e p

T t

L l

E e

P p

Who is staying healthy? Color the frame. Draw.

How do you stay healthy?

Values: We stay healthy.

✂ Cut out, listen, and paste.

Are You Okay?

1

2

3

4

Story Sequence: *Are You Okay?*

Count the stars and circle the number. Color.

20   21

22

23

24

25

26

27

28

29

Math Practice: *Numbers 20–29*

Look and circle the parts of the animals' bodies that protect them.

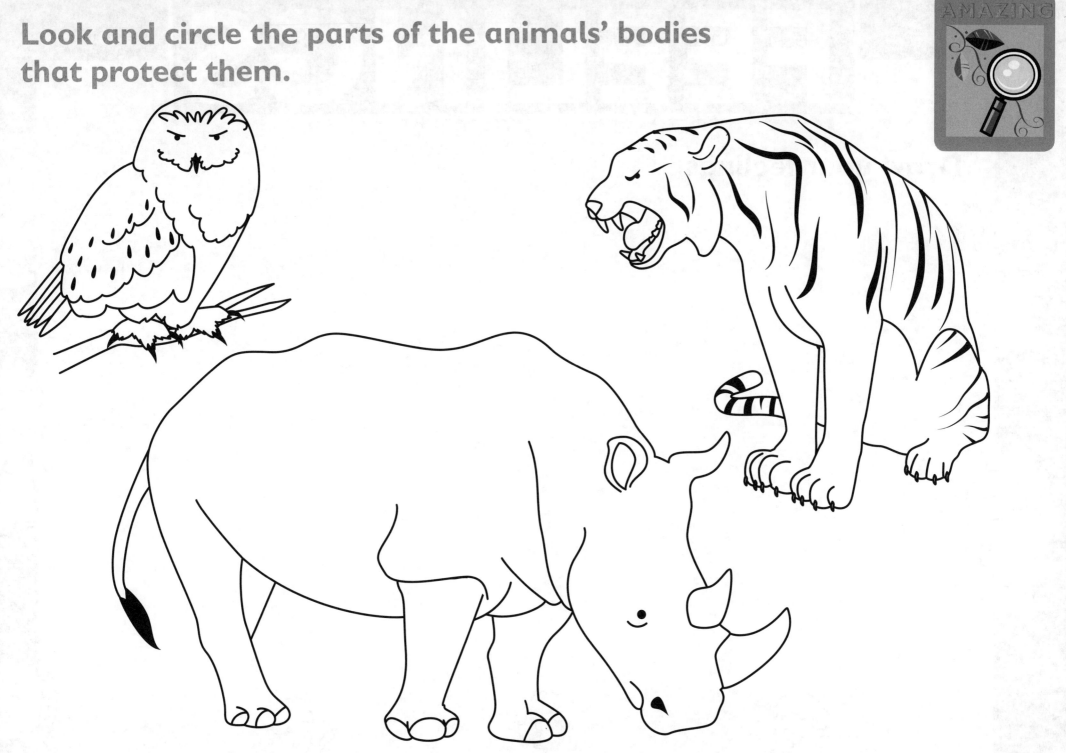

Amazing: Science Connection: *owl, claws; rhinoceros, horns; tiger, fangs/claws*

FEELINGS

Draw your feelings.

3 HOME

What is wrong? Find and circle.

Where are the family members? Look and match.

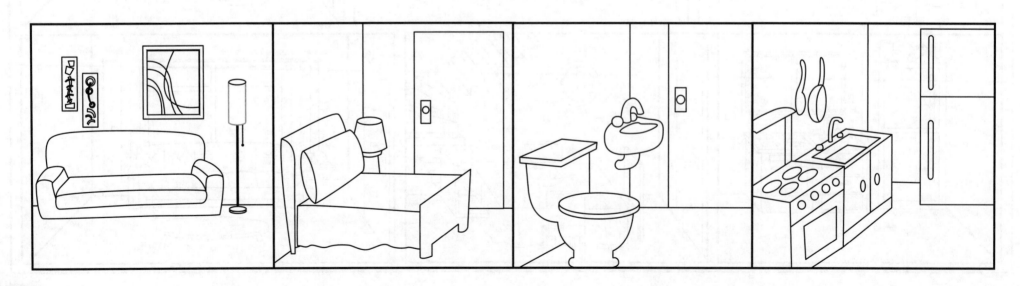

Vocabulary Practice and Review: family members; *living room, bedroom, bathroom, kitchen*

✂ **Cut out and paste. Say.**

Vocabulary Practice: *dining room, hallway, closet, stairs*
Language Practice: *Where is (the cat)? It's (in the closet).*

What is missing in each room? Trace, draw, and color.

Vocabulary Practice and Review: *kitchen, sink, stove, fridge, bedroom, bed, lamp, closet*

Trace and match.

C

n

N

g

I

c

G

i

Pre-reading and Pre-writing Practice: *Cc, Nn, Ii, Gg*, and discriminating sounds

VALUES Are they respecting differences? Complete the face. Trace and read the sentences.

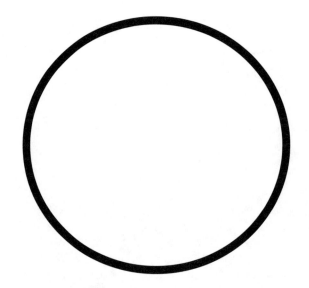

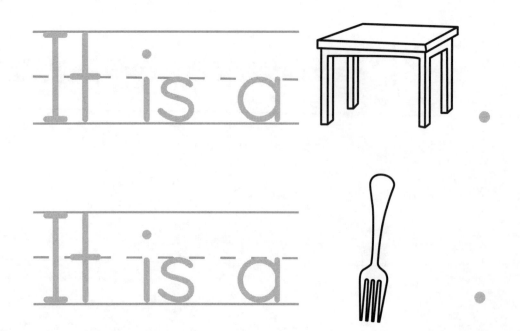

It is a [table].

It is a [fork].

Pre-reading and Pre-writing Practice: Rebuses and simple sentences; *table, fork*
Values: We respect differences.

Look and listen. Draw someone hiding in the box and say.

Where Is Meg?

Where is ... ?

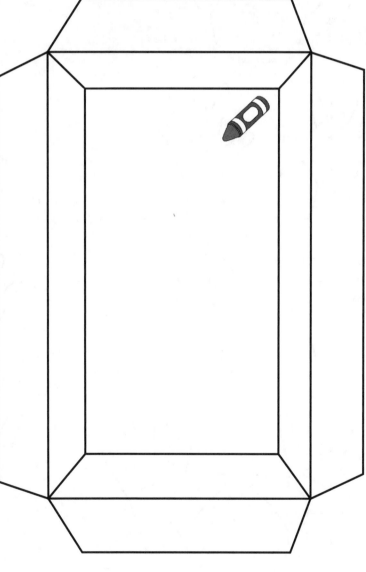

Circle the sets of ten fingers. Count and write.

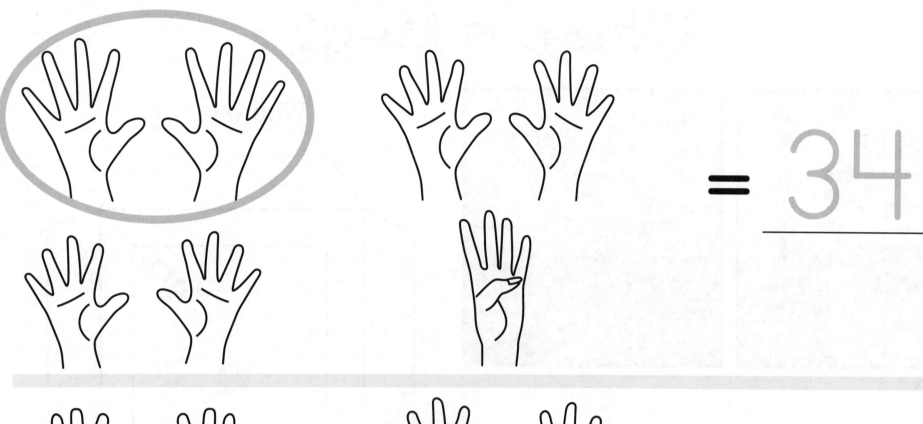

$= \underline{34}$

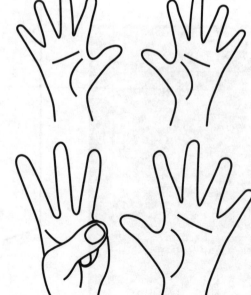

$= \underline{\hspace{2cm}}$

Math Practice: *Numbers 30–39*; sets of 10

What is for dinner? Circle an insect and draw it in the spider's web.

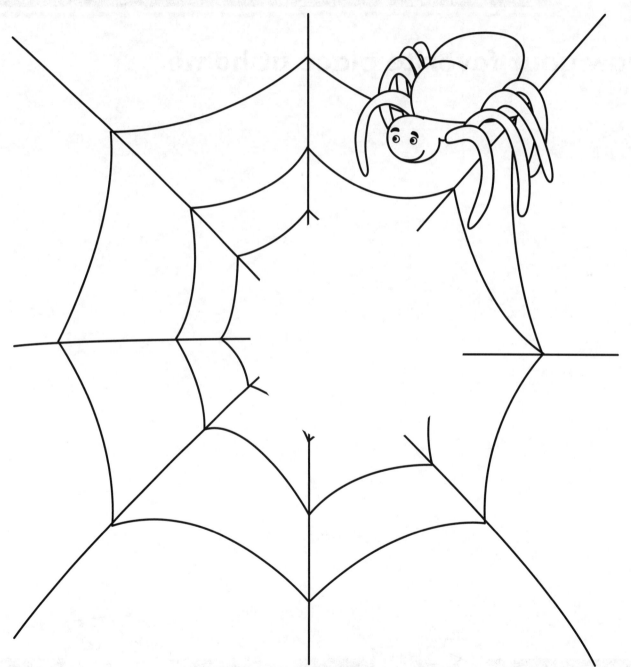

Amazing: Science Connection: *spider, web, butterfly, bee, fly*

HOME

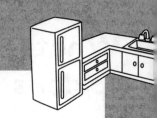

Draw your favorite place at home.

4 RECYCLE

What is wrong? Find and circle.

What do you need to make a wagon? Look and circle or cross out.

Vocabulary Practice: *tape, paper plates, box, string*

✂ **What do you need to make a kite?**
Cut out and paste.

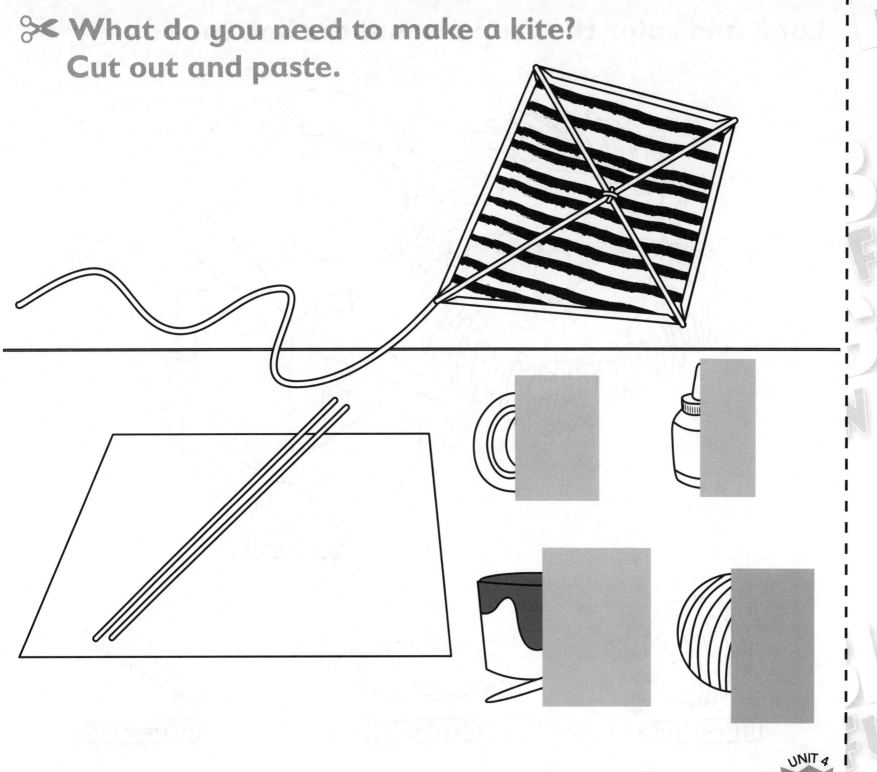

Vocabulary Practice: *paint, paintbrush, sticks, glue*
Vocabulary Review: *paper, tape, string*

Look and color the crayons and the lion mask.

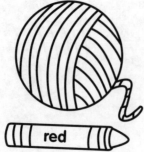
red

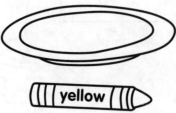
yellow

brown

Vocabulary Practice: *paper plate, string, stick;* colors

Trace and write. Trace, read, and circle. Trace, read, and draw.

H   R   B   O

h   r   b   o

It is a box.

It is a ring.

It is a hat.

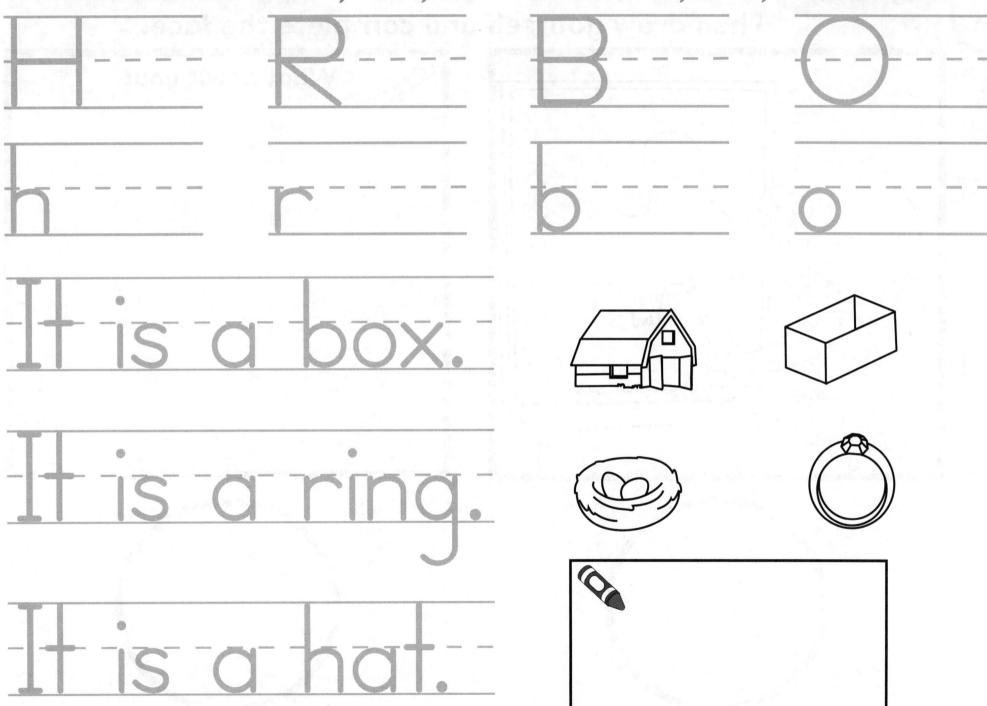

Pre-reading and Pre-writing Practice: *Hh, Rr, Bb, Oo*; simple sentences

Is he being wasteful? Draw a happy or a sad face. Then draw yourself and complete the face.

What about you?

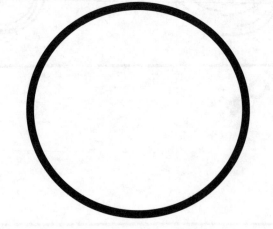

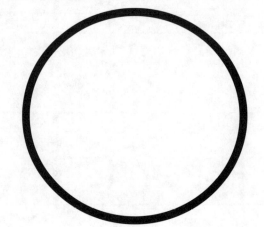

Values: We don't waste things.

 **Look and listen. Color what they need to make a tent.**

We Need Books!

What do they need?

Circle the sets of ten. Draw more flowers to match the numbers.

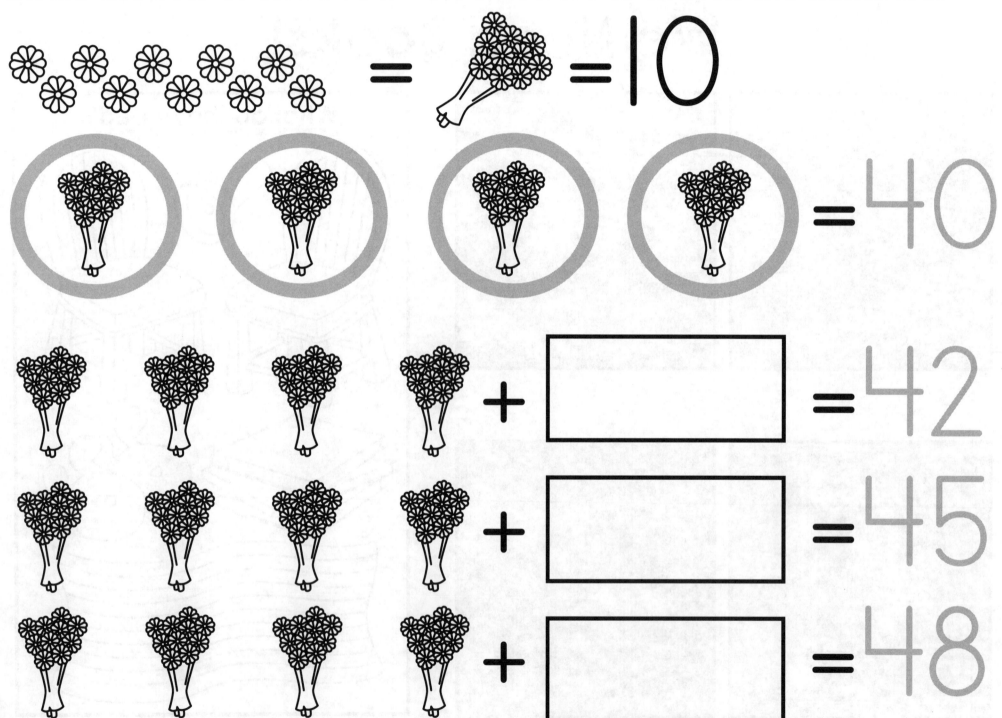

Math Practice: *Numbers 40–49*; sets of ten

Trace around the flying seeds. Match and color.

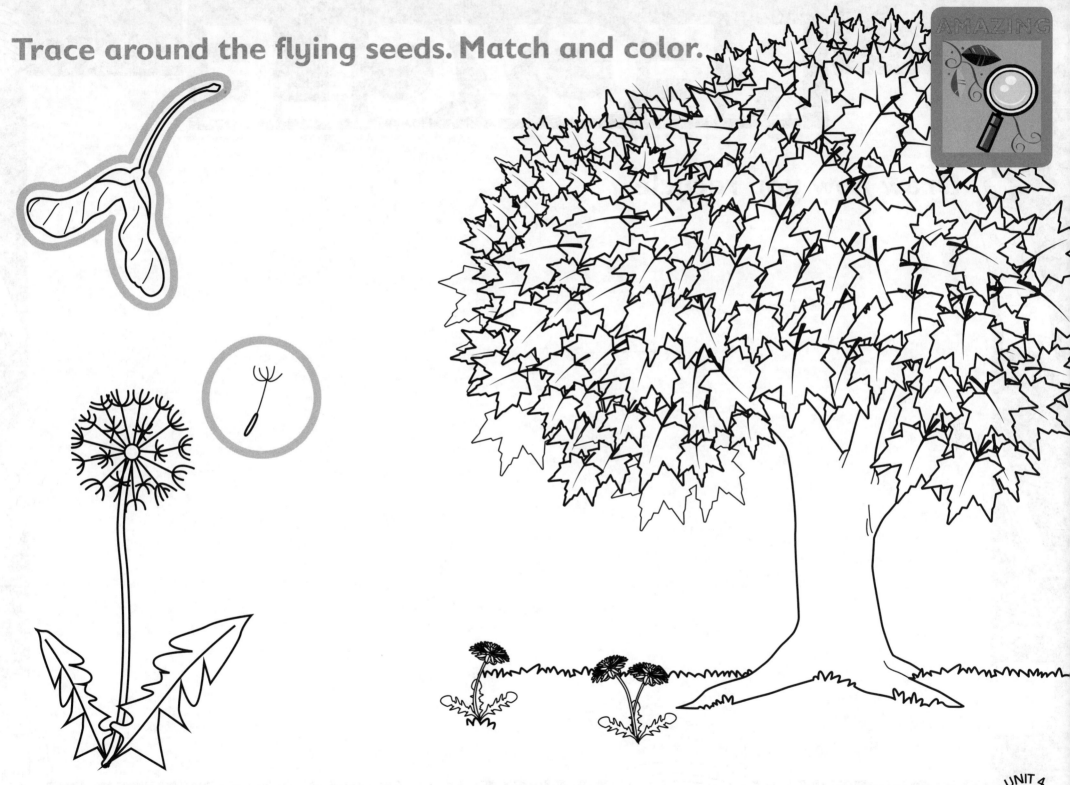

Amazing: Science Connection: *seeds, flowers, tree*

RECYCLE

Draw how you recycle.

5 EATING OUT

What is wrong? Find and circle.

What is each person missing? Look and match.

Vocabulary Practice: *menu, water, napkin, straw*

✂ **Cut out and paste. Color.**

Vocabulary Practice: *pizza, ice cream, cake, spaghetti*

What do you want to eat and drink? Draw and say.

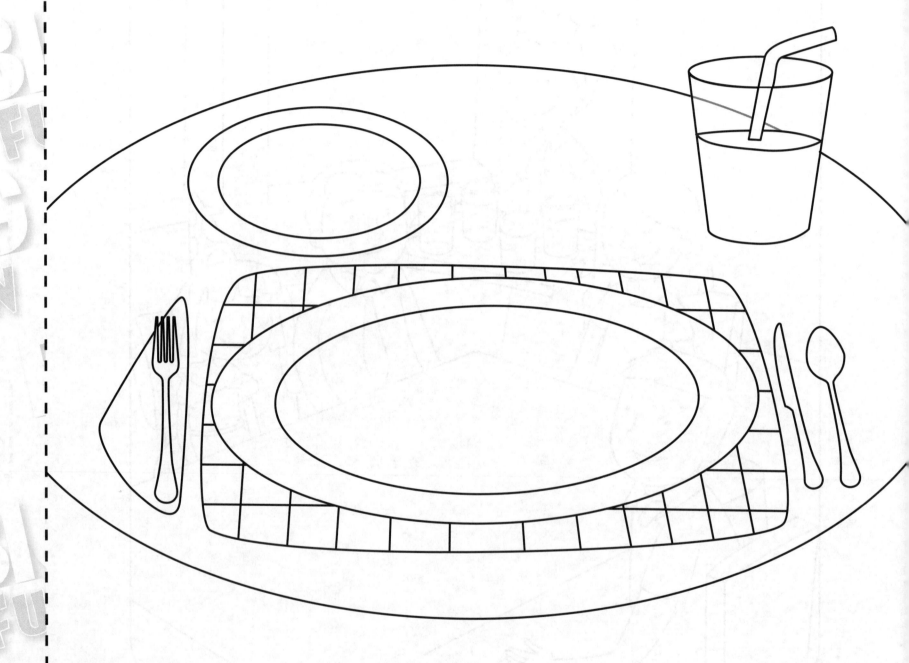

 Vocabulary Practice and Review: food; drinks; *napkin, straw*

Trace and match. Trace, write, and read.

K   D   U   J

j   d   k   u

It is a __uck.

It is a __acket.

VALUES

Who is helping others? Color the frame. Draw.

What about you?

Values: We help each other.

Look and listen. Color the food that Grandma orders.

Lunch with Grandma

What does Grandma order?

How old are they? Count and circle the correct speech bubbles.

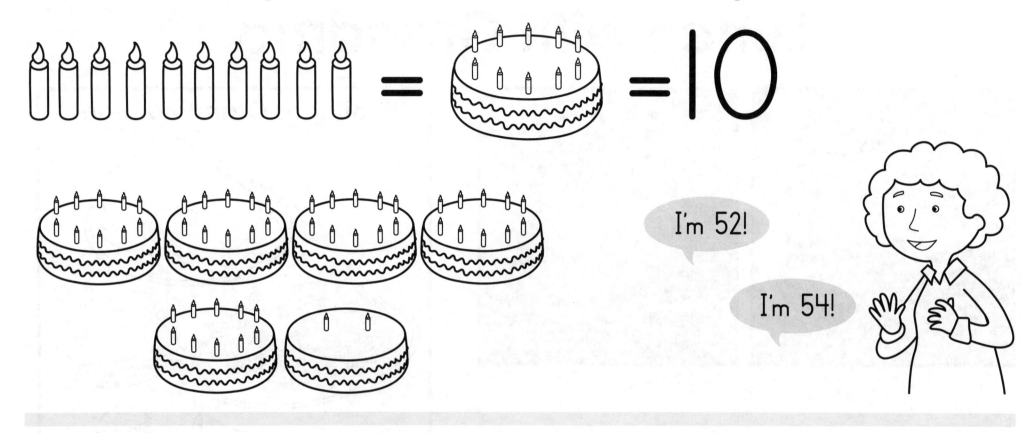

Math Practice: *Numbers 50–69; sets of ten*

Look at the patterns in the fruit and vegetables. Match.

 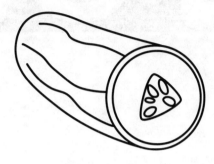  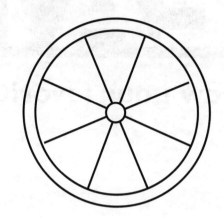

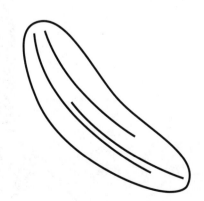 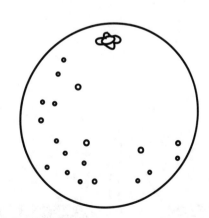  

EATING OUT

Draw your favorite restaurant.

6 OUR THINGS

What is wrong? Find and circle.

What is each person missing? Look and match.

Vocabulary Practice: *tablet, laptop, backpack, cell phone*

Look and circle the differences.

Trace, read, and color the corresponding item.

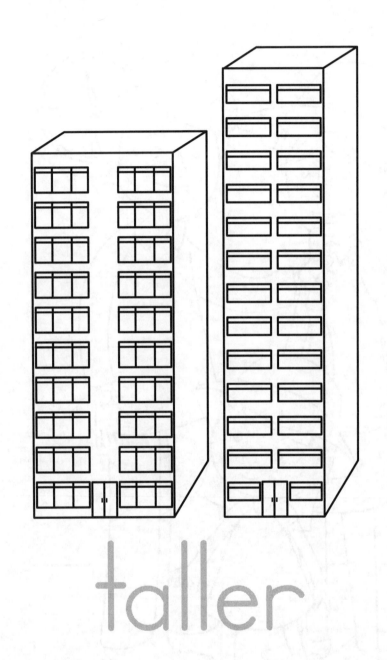

taller

bigger

longer

Vocabulary Practice: *taller, bigger, longer; building*
Vocabulary Review: *airplane, truck*

Trace and match. Then trace, read, and color.

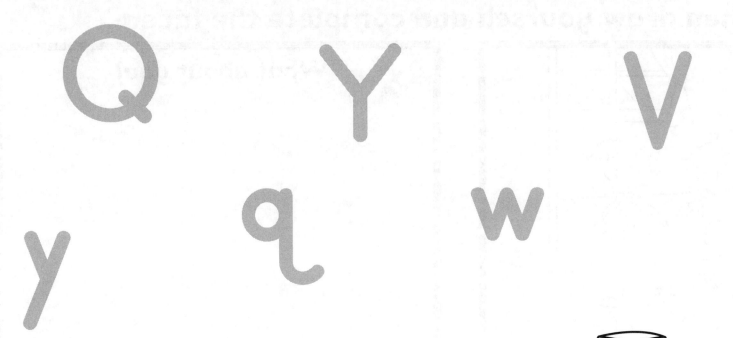

Q   Y   V   W

q   w   v

y

It is a red [vest].

It is a yellow [blanket].

Is she being neat? Look and draw a happy or a sad face. Then draw yourself and complete the face.

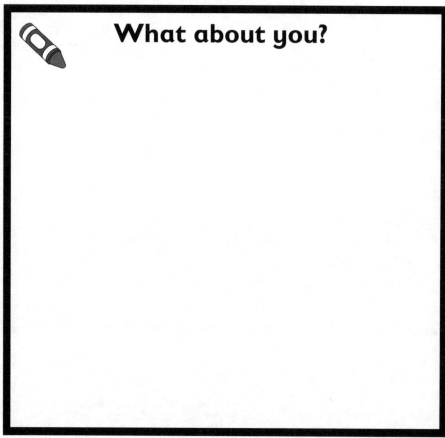

What about you?

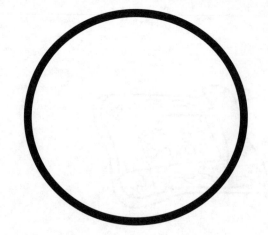

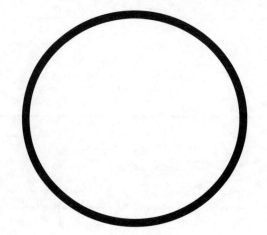

Values: We are neat.

Cut out, listen, and paste.

At the Store

1

2

3

4

Complete the number line. Count and answer.

70 71 __ 73 74 75 __ 77 __ 79

80 __ 82 83 __ 85 86 __ 88 89

=10

How many beads? ____

Math Practice: *Numbers 70–89; sets of ten*

Look and color by number.

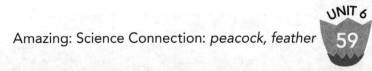

1 brown   2 green

3 blue   4 orange

Amazing: Science Connection: *peacock, feather*

OUR THINGS

Draw your favorite things.

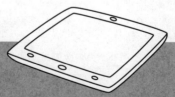

7 ANIMALS

What is wrong? Find and circle.

Look and match.

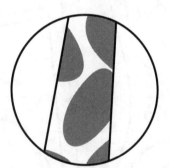

Vocabulary Practice: *tigers, seals, giraffes, kangaroos*

✂ **Cut out and paste.**

Vocabulary Practice: *monkeys, zebras, elephants, lions; sleeping, eating, playing, running*

Look and draw the morning, afternoon, and night sky. Then say what the zookeeper does.

morning   afternoon   night

Vocabulary Practice: zookeeper; morning, afternoon, night
Language Practice: *feeds the monkeys, sweeps the elephant exhibit, closes the zoo*

Trace and write. Trace, read, and circle.

X x   Z z

I see a zebra.

I see an ox.

I see a zoo.

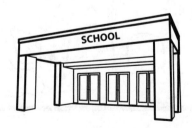 

VALUES

Who is working as a team? Color the frame. Draw.

How do you and your friends work as a team?

Values: We work as a team.

Look and listen. Draw what they see at the zoo.

At the Zoo

 What do they see at the zoo?

Connect the dots in number order. Name the animals.

Math Practice: *Numbers 1–90*

Circle the animals and plants that live underwater. Then draw more animals and plants and color.

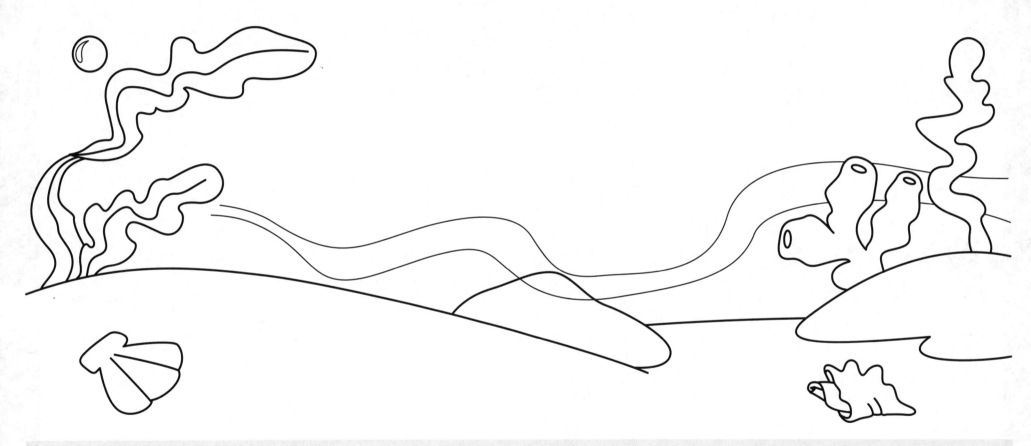

Amazing: Science Connection: *jellyfish, fish, coral, octopus*

ANIMALS

Draw your favorite wild animals.

8 PLACES

What is wrong? Find and circle.

Where do you want to go? Circle. Then draw yourself in that place.

   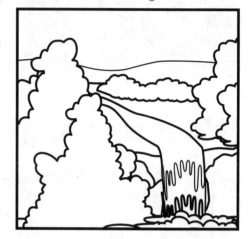

Vocabulary Practice: *beach, mountains, lake, stream*

✂ Cut out and paste.

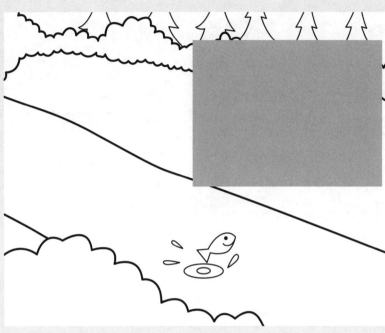

Vocabulary Practice: *fishing, camping, hiking, jogging; lake, stream, mountains, beach*

UNIT 8
73

Trace, read, and match.

1 ———————— first

2 ———————— then

3 ———————— last

 Vocabulary Practice: *first, then, last; build a campfire*

Trace and read. Look and number.

1. I see a big bird in a boat.

2. I see a big bear in a tent.

Is he sharing? Look and draw a happy or a sad face. Then draw yourself and complete the face.

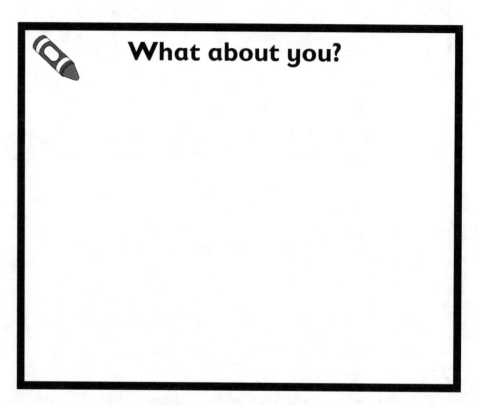

What about you?

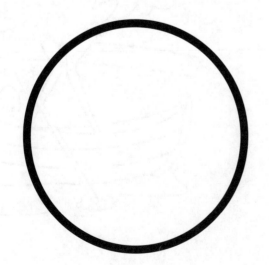

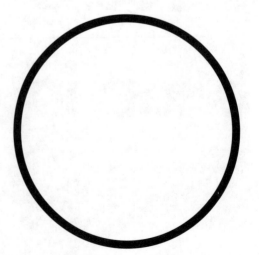

Look and listen. Color the animals that they see.

Camping

WHOOOOOOO

What do they see?

Trace and write the time. Then draw what you do at each time of the day.

7 o'clock   ___ o'clock   ___ o'clock

Math Practice: *Numbers 1-12*; telling time
Language Practice: *What time is it? It's (2) o'clock.*

Trace, read, and color. Draw.

first

then

last

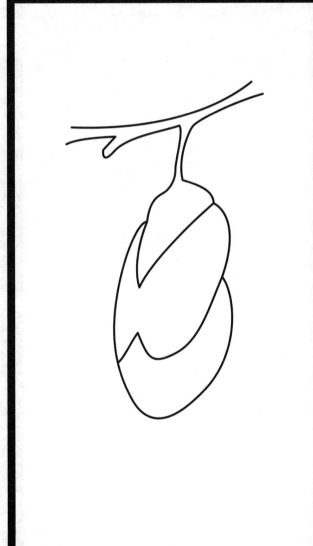

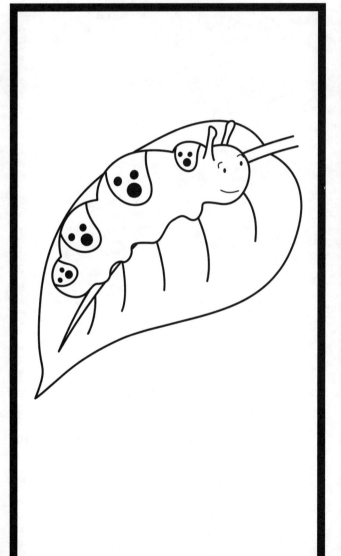

Amazing: Science Connection: *caterpillar, cocoon, butterfly*

PLACES

Draw yourself on vacation doing your favorite activity.

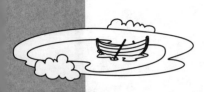

9 SHOW TIME!

Look and review.

Review Units 1–8: *music teacher, sleepy, bedroom/bed, paper plate/stick/string, cake, hat/necklace, giraffes/eating, lake/fishing*

Unit 1: Look and say. Who are they? What do they do?

Unit 2: Are you OK? Spin a crayon and say.

Unit 3: Name the places in the house. What are the boy and his cat doing?

Unit 4: Do you need... ? Spin a crayon and say.

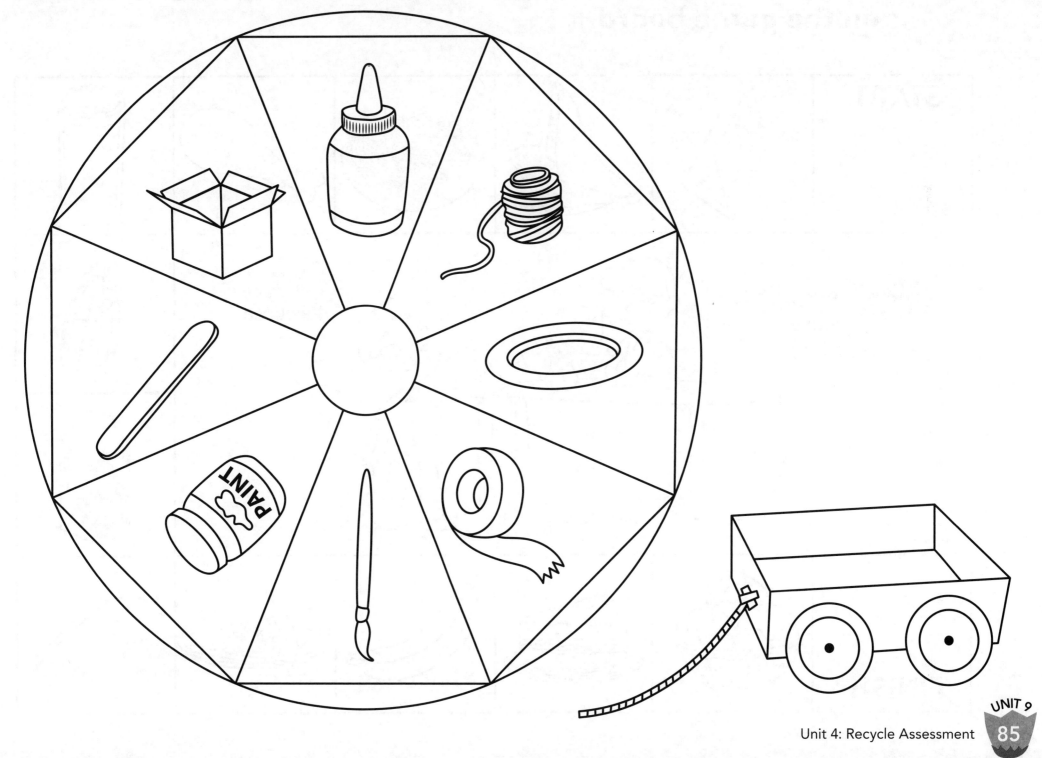

Unit 5: Play the Restaurant Game. Ask politely for the items on the game board.

Unit 6: **Where is the... ? Circle and say.**

Unit 7: Draw your path through the zoo. What do you see? What are the animals doing? Look and say.

ENTRANCE

EXIT

Unit 8: Where do you want to go? What can you do there? Point and say.

Workbook Audio CD

BIG FUN
WORKBOOK 3 Audio CD

has finished *Big Fun* Workbook 3!

Good job!

red yellow blue green
blue black
pink white
orange purple brown pink

has finished *Big Fun* **Workbook 3!**